This Twitter Workbook and Planner Belongs to:

If found, contact me here:

Phone: ______________________________

Email: ______________________________

Address ______________________________

**Dedicated To**

YOU and my clients



Published by
GreyChild Communications
Toronto, ON

Twitter Workbook and Planner / Dwainia Grey
ISBN-13: 978-0994888877

ISBN-10: 0994888872

# Introduction

## WHAT IS THIS?

This is the **Twitter Workbook and Planner** that will help you succeed with Twitter for your Empowerpreneur business. The book is based on the training in Awesome Nation Engagement; it's a companion book as well as a standalone workbook and planner. The Workbook Section of the book helps you create a Twitter strategy for the year and clarify your Twitter goals and tactics (action steps). The Planner Section of the book helps you plan your monthly Twitter strategy and track your monthly actions and milestones to get a clear picture of your Twitter Return on Investment (ROI).

By having a plan you leverage your time, reach targets (people and goals), add automation and measure success.

## HOW TO USE THIS WORKBOOK

The first part is the Strategy Workbook, which includes worksheets and checklists for you to complete. This helps you develop the Twitter Marketing Plan and success strategy for the coming months.

1. Objective
2. Audience
3. Style Guide
4. Engagement in 15 Minutes
5. Do's and Don'ts
6. Planning
7. Twitter Post Ideas
8. 52 Weeks
9. Twitter Profile Worksheet
10. Twitter Hashtags
11. Twitter Chat Schedule
12. Getting Started Cheat Sheet
13. Blog Stats
14. Twitter Yearly Stats

The second section is the **Twitter Action Planner**:

1. Monthly Calendar
2. Monthly Success Tracker
3. Monthly Stats
4. Status Updates
5. Twitter Campaign Planner
6. To Do
7. Notes

The planner section helps you plan your Twitter posts and engagement for the next 12 months. Each month includes monthly planning tools as well as metrics trackers. At the end of each month review the month and start planning for the new month. It's very important to complete your success tracker as it helps you to duplicate success.

The downloadable PDF contains 34 pages and allows you to print pages as needed.

## TWITTER TODAY

What is the biggest challenge that you are facing right now with Twitter?

What do you hope to accomplish?

What have you done so far to get your Twitter campaign started?

How much time do you currently spend on Twitter a week?

Are you directing Twitter followers to your email list?

Are you currently using any of the following tools?

- ☐ Twitter
- ☐ Linkedin
- ☐ Twitter
- ☐ YouTube
- ☐ Pinterest
- ☐ Google+
- ☐ Instagram
- ☐ Other sites

# twitter MARKETING WORKBOOK

# Objective



Objective Overall Twitter objective for the year.

- Increase reach
- Build your brand
- Engage influencers and connectors
- Increase customer loyalty
- Drive people to events
- Improve customer service
- Generate leads and sales
- Convert leads to sales

## Short-term

Goal # 1 –

Deadline

Action Plan

Goal Met ☐ Yes ☐NO

Goal # 2 –

Deadline

Action Plan

Goal Met ☐ Yes ☐NO

Goal # 3 –

Deadline

Action Plan

Goal Met ☐ Yes ☐NO

## Long-term

Goal –

Deadline

Action Plan

Goal Met ☐ Yes ☐NO

# Objective

twitter MARKETING

## Monthly Goal Setter

Set realistic achievable goals for each month.
Goals can be a number of posts or number of new followers to engagement. Make sure it's measurable.

| | |
|---|---|
| January | February |
| Goal Met ☐ Yes ☐NO | Goal Met ☐ Yes ☐NO |
| March | April |
| Goal Met ☐ Yes ☐NO | Goal Met ☐ Yes ☐NO |
| May | June |
| Goal Met ☐ Yes ☐NO | Goal Met ☐ Yes ☐NO |
| July | August |
| Goal Met ☐ Yes ☐NO | Goal Met ☐ Yes ☐NO |
| September | October |
| Goal Met ☐ Yes ☐NO | Goal Met ☐ Yes ☐NO |
| November | December |
| Goal Met ☐ Yes ☐NO | Goal Met ☐ Yes ☐NO |

# Audience



## Your Audience

- ☐ Existing clients
- ☐ Prospective clients

Where they are hanging out:

- ☐ Twitter
- ☐ Facebook
- ☐ Pinterest
- ☐ Instagram
- ☐ Google+
- ☐
- ☐
- ☐

## Who Are Your Competitors? – How Do They Use Facebook? – How Are You Different?

## What Keeps Your Client up at Night?

## How Does Your Product / Service Solve the Problem?

## List 3 Successes You Have Had with Clients
Think RESULTS

| What Words or Phrases Do Your Clients Use to Describe the Problem | What Words or Phrases Do Your Clients Use When They Are Looking for the Solution? (KEYWORDS) |
|---|---|
| | |

## Your Avatar

Name (fictitious):
Gender:
Age:
Profession:
Marital and Family Status:
Associations:
Location (city, neighborhood, or postal code):

# Style Guide

twitter MARKETING

## Image Text 1

Font
Size
Style
**Color**
Hex
RGB
CMYK

## Image Text 2

Font
Size
Style
**Color**
Hex
RGB
CMYK

## Watermark Text 1

Font
Size
Style
**Color**
Hex
RGB
CMYK

## Image Sizes

Profile 400 x 400 px
Background 1280 x 1024

## Header Image Template 1500 x 500 px

Use your header image for promotions and campaigns.

## Post Template 440 x 220 px

Show placement of graphics, watermark, text alignment, borders etc.

## Notes

Separate post templates for blog posts, quotes, promotions, etc?

Create templates using Photoshop, Fireworks, Canva or Picmonkey.

Voice, tone, offline topics, abbreviations, spellings and punctuation to use:

# 15 Minutes A Day of Engagement



| | Day 1 | Day 2 |
|---|---|---|
| 3-5 Minutes | **Retweet, favourite, and reply on other people's content.** | **Retweet, favourite, and reply on other people's content.** |
| 1-5 Minutes | **Notifications**<br>☐ Answer Comments (Good & Bad)<br>☐ Respond to Messages | **Notifications**<br>☐ Answer Comments (Good & Bad)<br>☐ Respond to Messages |
| 1-5 Minutes | **Start a Conversation**<br>@Mention someone in a post and/or send a DM (Direct Message) | **Make A New Friend**<br>☐ Influencers<br>☐ Current, Past & Future Clients<br>☐ Future Collaborators |

## WHEN THE MOOD STRIKES UPDATE YOUR STATUS

**Increase Engagement by Integrating Twitter on Your Website**

- ☐ Twitter Profile buttons
- ☐ Twitter Widget
- ☐ Tweet buttons
- ☐ Embed Twitter posts on blog posts

**Schedule**

- ☐ Schedule other peoples posts using scheduling tools
- ☐ Schedule your blog posts
- ☐ Day published
- ☐ 1 week later
- ☐ 1 month later

# Twitter Do's and Don'ts

twitter MARKETING

- [ ] Always follow the rules and regulations for Twitter. If you don't you can get your account suspended. Read the Twitter Page Terms.
- [ ] Do commit the time and effort to maintain your Twitter marketing plan.
- [ ] Don't be disrespectful, offensive, vulgar or use language considered to be inflammatory. Don't be rude or difficult to deal with when engaging with your followers
- [ ] Do create a social media marketing plan, but adjust your specific tactics as you go. Be flexible and take the time to find out what works and what doesn't work.
- [ ] Don't overdo it when promoting your business. You want to use Twitter to build relationships not overwhelm users with ads.
- [ ] Always include hashtags.
- [ ] Do listen to your clients through your Twitter account and respond promptly and where appropriate.
- [ ] Don't overuse hashtags
- [ ] Don't lie to your audience or hide the fact that you are advertising to them. Always be transparent with your intentions
- [ ] Do engage with people who have similar interests
- [ ] Don't just post your own content
- [ ] Do schedule tweets.
- [ ] Don't auto Direct Message
- [ ] Do use Twitter Ads
- [ ] Do support the promotional campaigns of other non-competitive businesses and your followers.
- [ ] Don't forget to add attribution when it's not your content. Use the @ tag
- [ ] Do participate – Join the conversation.
- [ ] Do pay attention to social media ethics
- [ ] Do pay attention to the metrics and analytics of your campaign.
- [ ] Do mention people and companies where appropriate
- [ ] Do use Twitter Cards for products, photos, post excerpts etc
- [ ] Do prepare to deal with how online users change, alter or use your brand's message. Have a plan for both good and bad customer feedback.
- [ ] Do tweet multiple times a day
- [ ] Do go local with Twitter, it's a great opportunity to take online relationships offline.
- [ ] Do answer all messages and mentions in a timely manner. Remember Twitter is real time.
- [ ] Do respond to non spammy mentions
- [ ] Do tweet other peoples content and mention them
- [ ] Don't spam!

# Twitter Do's and Don'ts



- ☐ **Do Use Twitter Lists**
  - ☐ Do create public lists of experts and influencers.
  - ☐ Do use public lists to find prospects
  - ☐ Do create targeted lists of clients, and influencers. Engage on a regular basis.
  - ☐ Do create private lists of industry influencers and your interests. Tweet, then retweet.
- ☐ **Do Use Twitter Search**
  - ☐ On a regular basis use search to find potential clients and people to follow by using key phrases (and words) used to find you.
  - ☐ Search your domain name to see if people are posting
  - ☐ Search misspellings of your Twitter handle, name, and business
  - ☐ Search using Hashtags

## Day-to-Day Management

How many times a week will you post on Twitter?
Suggested number of times a week to post: hourly

---

What days and times will you post?

---

How far ahead do you want to plan content?

---

How often will you promote your own content (blog posts, events, products and services) versus other peoples content?

---

What type of content are you going to share? Review the Post Idea Sheet. What you share needs to bring value - always think "What's in it for me?" Try for a combination of educating, and engaging. You are aiming to get them interested in you, your brand, and your business.

---

Who will create content? Images / Video / Copy

---

Who will post content?

---

Who will manage your Twitter campaigns?

---

Who will track, monitor, and report?

---

Number of people to follow each week:

---

How often will you engage in Twitter Chats?

---

# Planning

Do you want to assign posts to certain days a week? Throwback Thursday, Follow Friday, or make up your own

| | Themed Post | Create Content | Publish Content |
|---|---|---|---|
| Monday | | | |
| Tuesday | | | |
| Wednesday | | | |
| Thursday | | | |
| Friday | | | |
| Saturday | | | |
| Sunday | | | |

## Resources

- ☐ Experienced Writer
- ☐ Professional Photos / Photo shoot
- ☐ Professional Videos / Video shoot
- ☐ Branded Graphics

## Twitter Policy

Develop your Twitter Policy.
Read the Do's and Don'ts of Twitter. What are the policies you will have for your Empowerpreneur business?

- Rules of engagement
- How to handle customer service
- What to say and what not to say
- Workflow / Schedule
- How to handle negative feedback /criticism
    - Clients, media or competitors

## Budget

Startup and launch budget
Campaign budgets
Ongoing management budget
- Advertising
- Design
- Tools (Canva, Pic Monkey, Hootsuite, Buffer, etc)

## Metrics

Review your online metrics on a weekly and/or monthly basis. Use Google Analytics in conjunction with bitly, and the Twitter Insights to track and monitor your success. Also use Buffer and Hootsuite reporting tools.

Learn more about your return on investment (ROI – time and money) as well as which posts brings the most traffic, engagement and conversion.

Take time to complete the Blog Stats, Monthly Success Tracker and The Monthly And Yearly Social Media Stats.

# Va Va VooM™

## Va Va VooM ™ (Content Marketing Ratio)

Value – 60% - Tips, tutorials, and instructional useful and helpful posts

List 3 topics that you can post about that will add value

Visual – 20% - Make use of images and videos

List 3 ways you can use images / videos in social media

Voice – 10% - Show your personality – personal posts about you, showing your life, and a behind the scenes view

List 3 posts that will show your personality

Marketing – 10% - Promotional posts to sell and promote your products and services

List 3 products / services you want to sell / promote via social media

# Content Ideas for Twitter



| | | | | | | | |
|---|---|---|---|---|---|---|---|
| 1 | **Valuable and Useful Information** | 2 | **Blog Posts**<br>Ensure every blog has a branded image | 3 | **Influencers Posts** | 4 | **Personal Posts** |
| 5 | **Trending**<br>Get on the bandwagon and use trending hashtags. | 6 | **Twitter Chat**<br>Start or participate in a twitter chat | 7 | **Twitter Exclusives**<br>Twitter only events, products, and promotions | 8 | **Events, Workshops and Seminars**<br>Share online and offline events you are hosting or attending |
| 9 | **Your Work**<br>Post updates about your work | 10 | **Emotional / funny posts** | 11 | **Testimonials**<br>Post client testimonials and tag them | 12 | **Business News**<br>Updates about your business and industry. |
| 13 | **Quotes**<br>Post quotes that will motivate and inspire your audience. | 14 | **Products / Services**<br>Links and, images to your products and services | 15 | **Video / Photos**<br>Pictures of you and your products | 16 | **Questions / Poll**<br>Ask the community what they think<br><br>Answer questions |
| 17 | **Promotions**<br>Promote your products, services, sales and coupons. Use contests, giveaways and sweepstakes | 18 | **Contests** | 19 | **Breaking News**<br>Updates in your industry / niche. | 20 | **Celebrate Milestones / Anniversaries**<br>Almost at 1,000 followers? |

# 52 Weeks

Plan out 52 weeks of Tips, Quotes, etc
52 Weeks of ___________________________

| | | | |
|---|---|---|---|
| 1 | | 27 | |
| 2 | | 28 | |
| 3 | | 29 | |
| 4 | | 30 | |
| 5 | | 31 | |
| 6 | | 32 | |
| 7 | | 33 | |
| 8 | | 34 | |
| 9 | | 35 | |
| 10 | | 36 | |
| 11 | | 37 | |
| 12 | | 38 | |
| 13 | | 39 | |
| 14 | | 40 | |
| 15 | | 41 | |
| 16 | | 42 | |
| 17 | | 43 | |
| 18 | | 44 | |
| 19 | | 45 | |
| 20 | | 46 | |
| 21 | | 47 | |
| 22 | | 48 | |
| 23 | | 49 | |
| 24 | | 50 | |
| 25 | | 51 | |
| 26 | | 52 | |

# Twitter Profile

twitter MARKETING

- ☐ Branded Header Image
- ☐ Professional Profile Image
- ☐ Name – Use your real name
- ☐ Bio – Branded, search optimized profile (160 Characters)
- ☐ Location
- ☐ Website URL
- ☐ Birthday

## Optimized Bio

# Hashtags

twitter MARKETING

| #Hashtags to Use | ✓ |
|---|---|
| | |
| | |
| | |
| | |
| | |
| | |
| | |
| | |
| | |
| | |
| | |
| | |
| | |
| | |
| | |
| | |
| | |
| | |
| | |
| | |
| | |
| | |
| | |
| | |
| | |
| | |
| | |

Use hashtags. List popular hashtags for your preferred client, industry, and niche. Create hashtags for your business, and products and services.

# Chat Schedule

twitter MARKETING

| Twitter Chats | Date | Time | ✓ |
|---|---|---|---|
| # | | | |
| # | | | |
| # | | | |
| # | | | |
| # | | | |
| # | | | |
| # | | | |
| # | | | |
| # | | | |
| # | | | |
| # | | | |
| # | | | |
| # | | | |
| # | | | |
| # | | | |
| # | | | |
| # | | | |
| # | | | |
| # | | | |
| # | | | |
| # | | | |
| # | | | |
| # | | | |
| # | | | |
| # | | | |
| # | | | |
| # | | | |

# Getting Started Cheat Sheet twitter MARKETING

## Branding

- ☐ I have a clear description of who my target audience is.
- ☐ My preferred client is using Twitter.
- ☐ I have included a professional photo or logo on my Twitter profile?
- ☐ My Twitter name is easy to find, follow, and connect with.
  - ☐ It's my name, business name, brand name or based on an SEO keyword.
  - ☐ It's the same as my other social media profile names for consistency
- ☐ I have a completed Twitter Page with a profile image, and branded header?
- ☐ Bio section includes keywords and website URL and reflects my voice and brand
- ☐ I know what personality/ brand message and image I want to communicate.
- ☐ I have included a professional email address - @yourwebsite.com
- ☐ I have included my business location (where applicable - at least put country)
- ☐ I link to other social media profiles (where applicable)

## Planning

- ☐ I know my Twitter objective
- ☐ I have defined my Twitter marketing goals and know how I will track them.
- ☐ I've created systems to test and track my social media marketing goals and tactics.
- ☐ I have a *Social Media Marketing Plan* that I use to help guide my online marketing and I've integrated my Twitter marketing tactics into my overall social media marketing strategies.
- ☐ I've use relevant dashboards and automation tools such as Hootsuite to optimize my time.
- ☐ I've documented the systems and tools I use, so it can be easily delegated.
- ☐ I use Twitter Analytics to create targeted posts and know the best day and time for engagement
- ☐ I use Twitter Advertising
- ☐ I have a (monthly/ weekly / daily) posting schedule for Twitter
- ☐ I have a (monthly/ weekly/ daily) Twitter engagement schedule
  - ☐ Post Status Updates
  - ☐ Respond to all messages and comments
  - ☐ Mention people when you post their content
- ☐ I have a strategy to capture leads from Twitter and to get followers to buy

# Getting Started Cheat Sheet

twitter MARKETING

## Content

- ☐ I have developed a system to find valuable content to share on Twitter
- ☐ I make sure I share a good mix of content (*Va Va VooM* – Value, Voice, Visual and Marketing)
- ☐ I use a Call To Action in posts
- ☐ I'm creating specific promotions and offers for my Twitter audience - *EXCLUSIVE.*
- ☐ I periodically change my Twitter cover photo to highlight my products / services, product launches and promotions
- ☐ I use an editorial calendar to layout content for my blog, and Twitter posts.
- ☐ I schedule blog posts as they are published, a week later, and a month later.
- ☐ I create a schedule to promote old blog posts.
- ☐ I use Twitter Analytics to find the optimal day and time to post content for maximum engagement
- ☐ I follow the top blogs in my industry to stay on top of trends.
- ☐ I create specific content to share on Twitter
- ☐ I always check for grammar and spelling

## Twitter Tools

- ☐ Twitter Analytics
- ☐ Followonk
- ☐ TweetDeck
- ☐ Hootsuite
- ☐ Buffer
- ☐ Canva
- ☐ Picmonkey
- ☐ Pixlr

# Blog Stats



| | Date | Twitter | Facebook | Google+ | Pinterest | Instagram | Blog Visits |
|---|---|---|---|---|---|---|---|
| | | | | | | | |
| 1 | | | | | | | |
| 2 | | | | | | | |
| 3 | | | | | | | |
| 4 | | | | | | | |
| 5 | | | | | | | |
| 6 | | | | | | | |
| 7 | | | | | | | |
| 8 | | | | | | | |
| 9 | | | | | | | |
| 10 | | | | | | | |
| 11 | | | | | | | |
| 12 | | | | | | | |
| 13 | | | | | | | |
| 14 | | | | | | | |
| 15 | | | | | | | |
| 16 | | | | | | | |
| 17 | | | | | | | |
| 18 | | | | | | | |
| 19 | | | | | | | |
| 20 | | | | | | | |
| 21 | | | | | | | |
| 22 | | | | | | | |
| 23 | | | | | | | |
| 24 | | | | | | | |
| 25 | | | | | | | |
| 26 | | | | | | | |
| 27 | | | | | | | |
| 28 | | | | | | | |
| 29 | | | | | | | |
| 30 | | | | | | | |
| 31 | | | | | | | |
| 32 | | | | | | | |
| 33 | | | | | | | |
| 34 | | | | | | | |
| 35 | | | | | | | |
| 36 | | | | | | | |
| 37 | | | | | | | |
| 38 | | | | | | | |
| 39 | | | | | | | |
| 40 | | | | | | | |
| 41 | | | | | | | |
| 42 | | | | | | | |
| 43 | | | | | | | |
| 44 | | | | | | | |
| 45 | | | | | | | |
| 46 | | | | | | | |
| 47 | | | | | | | |
| 48 | | | | | | | |
| 49 | | | | | | | |
| 50 | | | | | | | |
| 51 | | | | | | | |
| 52 | | | | | | | |

# Yearly Stats



| Year | Total Followers | | # of Retweets | | # of Posts | | # of Favourites | | # of Comments | | # of Clicks to Website | |
|---|---|---|---|---|---|---|---|---|---|---|---|---|
| | Goal | Actual | Goal | Actual | Goal | Actual | Goal | Actual | Goal | Actual | Goal | Actual |
| **January** | | | | | | | | | | | | |
| **February** | | | | | | | | | | | | |
| **March** | | | | | | | | | | | | |
| **April** | | | | | | | | | | | | |
| **May** | | | | | | | | | | | | |
| **June** | | | | | | | | | | | | |
| **July** | | | | | | | | | | | | |
| **August** | | | | | | | | | | | | |
| **September** | | | | | | | | | | | | |
| **October** | | | | | | | | | | | | |
| **November** | | | | | | | | | | | | |
| **December** | | | | | | | | | | | | |
| **Yearly Total** | | | | | | | | | | | | |

# twitter
# MARKETING
## PLANNER

# Editorial Calendar

twitter MARKETING

## Month

| SUNDAY | MONDAY | TUESDAY | WEDNESDAY | THURSDAY | FRIDAY | SATURDAY |
|---|---|---|---|---|---|---|
| | | | | | | |
| | | | | | | |
| | | | | | | |
| | | | | | | |
| | | | | | | |

## Notes

## Acknowledge and Celebrate Your Success

Month:

---

Total Followers

---

Post with most engagement (Retweets, Favorites, and Replies) on Twitter

---

Post with most clicks

---

Blog post with most traffic from Twitter

---

This month I learned

---

A record I broke this month

---

My celebration this month

---

Next month I plan to do the same

---

Next month I plan to try (new)

---

# Monthly Stats

**GOAL:**

| Total Followers | New Followers | # of Posts | # of Retweets | # of Favorites | # of Comments | # of Mentions | # of Clicks | # of Clicks to Website |
|---|---|---|---|---|---|---|---|---|
| | | | | | | | | |

| | |
|---|---|
| **EMAIL SUBSCRIBERS FROM TWITTER** | |

| | |
|---|---|
| **ENGAGEMENT** | |
| **Post with most retweets** | |
| **Post with most favorites** | |
| **Post with most comments** | |
| **Post with most clicks** | |

| | | | |
|---|---|---|---|
| **TWITTER ADS** | | | |
| Spend $ | | Results | |

# Status Updates



| Twitter Status Updates | Date | Time | ✓ |
|---|---|---|---|
| | | | |
| | | | |
| | | | |
| | | | |
| | | | |
| | | | |
| | | | |
| | | | |
| | | | |
| | | | |
| | | | |
| | | | |
| | | | |
| | | | |
| | | | |
| | | | |
| | | | |
| | | | |
| | | | |
| | | | |
| | | | |
| | | | |
| | | | |
| | | | |
| | | | |
| | | | |
| | | | |

# Product / Service Campaign

| | |
|---|---|
| Campaign | |
| Description | |
| Product / Service Newsletter<br>Contest / Giveaway | |
| Start | End |
| Objective | |
| Target Audience | |
| Budget$ / Cost$ / Return$ | |
| Landing Page | |
| Tracking Link | |
| Days and Time | |
| Winner / Date Notified | |

Image

- ☐ Blog Post Announcement
- ☐ Blog Post Follow-up
- ☐ Autoresponder Setup
- ☐ Ad Campaign
  - Budget$
  - Cost$
  - Return$
  - Click Thru Rate
  - CPC (Cost per Click)
- ☐ Conversion Rate
- ☐ Hashtag
- ☐ Coupon Code (if applicable)

# Advertising Campaign

| | |
|---|---|
| Campaign | |
| Boost / Ad | |
| Description | |
| Start | End |
| Objective | |
| Target Audience | |
| Budget$ / Cost Per Day$ | |
| Landing Page | |
| Tracking Link | |

Text

Demographic

Image

# To Do

twitter MARKETING

| | Priority | Completed |
|---|---|---|
| | | |
| | | |
| | | |
| | | |
| | | |
| | | |
| | | |
| | | |
| | | |
| | | |
| | | |
| | | |
| | | |
| | | |
| | | |
| | | |
| | | |
| | | |
| | | |
| | | |
| | | |
| | | |

## Month

| SUNDAY | MONDAY | TUESDAY | WEDNESDAY | THURSDAY | FRIDAY | SATURDAY |
|---|---|---|---|---|---|---|
| | | | | | | |
| | | | | | | |
| | | | | | | |
| | | | | | | |
| | | | | | | |

## Notes

# Success Tracker

twitter MARKETING

## Acknowledge and Celebrate Your Success

Month:

---

Total Followers

---

Post with most engagement (Retweets, Favorites, and Replies) on Twitter

---

Post with most clicks

---

Blog post with most traffic from Twitter

---

This month I learned

---

A record I broke this month

---

My celebration this month

---

Next month I plan to do the same

---

Next month I plan to try (new)

---

# Monthly Stats



GOAL:

| Total Followers | New Followers | # of Posts | # of Retweets | # of Favorites | # of Comments | # of Mentions | # of Clicks | # of Clicks to Website |
|---|---|---|---|---|---|---|---|---|
| | | | | | | | | |

| | |
|---|---|
| **EMAIL SUBSCRIBERS FROM TWITTER** | |
| **ENGAGEMENT** | |
| **Post with most retweets** | |
| **Post with most favorites** | |
| **Post with most comments** | |
| **Post with most clicks** | |
| **TWITTER ADS** | |

| | | | |
|---|---|---|---|
| Spend $ | | Results | |

# Status Updates



| Twitter Status Updates | Date | Time | ✓ |
|---|---|---|---|
| | | | |
| | | | |
| | | | |
| | | | |
| | | | |
| | | | |
| | | | |
| | | | |
| | | | |
| | | | |
| | | | |
| | | | |
| | | | |
| | | | |
| | | | |
| | | | |
| | | | |
| | | | |
| | | | |
| | | | |
| | | | |
| | | | |
| | | | |
| | | | |
| | | | |
| | | | |
| | | | |

# Product / Service Campaign

| | |
|---|---|
| Campaign | |
| Description | |
| Product / Service Newsletter<br>Contest / Giveaway | |
| Start | End |
| Objective | |
| Target Audience | |
| Budget$ / Cost$ / Return$ | |
| Landing Page | |
| Tracking Link | |
| Days and Time | |
| Winner / Date Notified | |

| Image |
|---|
| |

- ☐ Blog Post Announcement
- ☐ Blog Post Follow-up
- ☐ Autoresponder Setup
- ☐ Ad Campaign
  - Budget$
  - Cost$
  - Return$
  - Click Thru Rate
  - CPC (Cost per Click)
- ☐ Conversion Rate
- ☐ Hashtag
- ☐ Coupon Code (if applicable)

# Advertising Campaign

| | |
|---|---|
| Campaign | |
| Boost / Ad | |
| Description | |
| Start | End |
| Objective | |
| Target Audience | |
| Budget$ / Cost Per Day$ | |
| Landing Page | |
| Tracking Link | |

Text

Demographic

Image

# To Do



| | Priority | Completed |
|---|---|---|
| | | |
| | | |
| | | |
| | | |
| | | |
| | | |
| | | |
| | | |
| | | |
| | | |
| | | |
| | | |
| | | |
| | | |
| | | |
| | | |
| | | |
| | | |
| | | |
| | | |
| | | |
| | | |

# Editorial Calendar

twitter MARKETING

## Month

| SUNDAY | MONDAY | TUESDAY | WEDNESDAY | THURSDAY | FRIDAY | SATURDAY |
|---|---|---|---|---|---|---|
| | | | | | | |
| | | | | | | |
| | | | | | | |
| | | | | | | |
| | | | | | | |

## Notes

# Success Tracker

twitter MARKETING

## Acknowledge and Celebrate Your Success

Month:

---

Total Followers

---

Post with most engagement (Retweets, Favorites, and Replies) on Twitter

---

Post with most clicks

---

Blog post with most traffic from Twitter

---

This month I learned

---

A record I broke this month

---

My celebration this month

---

Next month I plan to do the same

---

Next month I plan to try (new)

---

# Monthly Stats

GOAL:

| Total Followers | New Followers | # of Posts | # of Retweets | # of Favorites | # of Comments | # of Mentions | # of Clicks | # of Clicks to Website |
|---|---|---|---|---|---|---|---|---|
| | | | | | | | | |

| | |
|---|---|
| **EMAIL SUBSCRIBERS FROM TWITTER** | |
| **ENGAGEMENT** | |
| **Post with most retweets** | |
| **Post with most favorites** | |
| **Post with most comments** | |
| **Post with most clicks** | |
| **TWITTER ADS** | |

| | | | |
|---|---|---|---|
| Spend $ | | Results | |

# Status Updates

| Twitter Status Updates | Date | Time | ✓ |
|---|---|---|---|
| | | | |
| | | | |
| | | | |
| | | | |
| | | | |
| | | | |
| | | | |
| | | | |
| | | | |
| | | | |
| | | | |
| | | | |
| | | | |
| | | | |
| | | | |
| | | | |
| | | | |
| | | | |
| | | | |
| | | | |
| | | | |
| | | | |
| | | | |
| | | | |
| | | | |
| | | | |
| | | | |

# Campaign Manager

twitter MARKETING

## Product / Service Campaign

| | |
|---|---|
| Campaign | |
| Description | |
| Product / Service Newsletter<br>Contest / Giveaway | |
| Start | End |
| Objective | |
| Target Audience | |
| Budget$ / Cost$ / Return$ | |
| Landing Page | |
| Tracking Link | |
| Days and Time | |
| Winner / Date Notified | |

| Image |
|---|
| |

- ☐ Blog Post Announcement
- ☐ Blog Post Follow-up
- ☐ Autoresponder Setup
- ☐ Ad Campaign
    - ○ Budget$
    - ○ Cost$
    - ○ Return$
    - ○ Click Thru Rate
    - ○ CPC (Cost per Click)
- ☐ Conversion Rate
- ☐ Hashtag
- ☐ Coupon Code (if applicable)

# Campaign Manager

twitter MARKETING

## Advertising Campaign

| | |
|---|---|
| Campaign | |
| Boost / Ad | |
| Description | |
| Start | End |
| Objective | |
| Target Audience | |
| Budget$ / Cost Per Day$ | |
| Landing Page | |
| Tracking Link | |

| Text | Demographic |
|---|---|
| | |

| Image |
|---|
| |

# To Do

| | Priority | Completed |
|---|---|---|
| | | |
| | | |
| | | |
| | | |
| | | |
| | | |
| | | |
| | | |
| | | |
| | | |
| | | |
| | | |
| | | |
| | | |
| | | |
| | | |
| | | |
| | | |
| | | |
| | | |
| | | |
| | | |

# Notes

# Editorial Calendar

twitter MARKETING

## Month

| SUNDAY | MONDAY | TUESDAY | WEDNESDAY | THURSDAY | FRIDAY | SATURDAY |
|---|---|---|---|---|---|---|
| | | | | | | |
| | | | | | | |
| | | | | | | |
| | | | | | | |
| | | | | | | |

## Notes

# Success Tracker

twitter MARKETING

## Acknowledge and Celebrate Your Success

Month:

Total Followers

Post with most engagement (Retweets, Favorites, and Replies) on Twitter

Post with most clicks

Blog post with most traffic from Twitter

This month I learned

A record I broke this month

My celebration this month

Next month I plan to do the same

Next month I plan to try (new)

# Monthly Stats



GOAL:

| Total Followers | New Followers | # of Posts | # of Retweets | # of Favorites | # of Comments | # of Mentions | # of Clicks | # of Clicks to Website |
|---|---|---|---|---|---|---|---|---|
| | | | | | | | | |

| | |
|---|---|
| **EMAIL SUBSCRIBERS FROM TWITTER** | |
| **ENGAGEMENT** | |
| **Post with most retweets** | |
| **Post with most favorites** | |
| **Post with most comments** | |
| **Post with most clicks** | |
| **TWITTER ADS** | |

| | | | |
|---|---|---|---|
| Spend $ | | Results | |

# Status Updates

| Twitter Status Updates | Date | Time | ✓ |
|---|---|---|---|
| | | | |
| | | | |
| | | | |
| | | | |
| | | | |
| | | | |
| | | | |
| | | | |
| | | | |
| | | | |
| | | | |
| | | | |
| | | | |
| | | | |
| | | | |
| | | | |
| | | | |
| | | | |
| | | | |
| | | | |
| | | | |
| | | | |
| | | | |
| | | | |
| | | | |
| | | | |
| | | | |

# Product / Service Campaign

| | |
|---|---|
| Campaign | |
| Description | |
| Product / Service Newsletter<br>Contest / Giveaway | |
| Start | End |
| Objective | |
| Target Audience | |
| Budget$ / Cost$ / Return$ | |
| Landing Page | |
| Tracking Link | |
| Days and Time | |
| Winner / Date Notified | |

| Image |
|---|
| |

- ☐ Blog Post Announcement
- ☐ Blog Post Follow-up
- ☐ Autoresponder Setup
- ☐ Ad Campaign
  - Budget$
  - Cost$
  - Return$
  - Click Thru Rate
  - CPC (Cost per Click)
- ☐ Conversion Rate
- ☐ Hashtag
- ☐ Coupon Code (if applicable)

## Advertising Campaign

| | |
|---|---|
| Campaign | |
| Boost / Ad | |
| Description | |
| Start | End |
| Objective | |
| Target Audience | |
| Budget$ / Cost Per Day$ | |
| Landing Page | |
| Tracking Link | |

| Text |
|---|
| |

| Demographic |
|---|
| |

| Image |
|---|
| |

# To Do

| | Priority | Completed |
|---|---|---|
| | | |
| | | |
| | | |
| | | |
| | | |
| | | |
| | | |
| | | |
| | | |
| | | |
| | | |
| | | |
| | | |
| | | |
| | | |
| | | |
| | | |
| | | |
| | | |
| | | |
| | | |

# Editorial Calendar



## Month

| SUNDAY | MONDAY | TUESDAY | WEDNESDAY | THURSDAY | FRIDAY | SATURDAY |
|---|---|---|---|---|---|---|
| | | | | | | |
| | | | | | | |
| | | | | | | |
| | | | | | | |
| | | | | | | |

## Notes

## Acknowledge and Celebrate Your Success

Month:

---

Total Followers

---

Post with most engagement (Retweets, Favorites, and Replies) on Twitter

---

Post with most clicks

---

Blog post with most traffic from Twitter

---

This month I learned

---

A record I broke this month

---

My celebration this month

---

Next month I plan to do the same

---

Next month I plan to try (new)

---

# Monthly Stats



GOAL:

| Total Followers | New Followers | # of Posts | # of Retweets | # of Favorites | # of Comments | # of Mentions | # of Clicks | # of Clicks to Website |
|---|---|---|---|---|---|---|---|---|
| | | | | | | | | |

| | |
|---|---|
| **EMAIL SUBSCRIBERS FROM TWITTER** | |
| **ENGAGEMENT** | |
| **Post with most retweets** | |
| **Post with most favorites** | |
| **Post with most comments** | |
| **Post with most clicks** | |
| **TWITTER ADS** | |

| | | | |
|---|---|---|---|
| Spend $ | | Results | |

# Status Updates



| Twitter Status Updates | Date | Time | ✓ |
|---|---|---|---|
| | | | |
| | | | |
| | | | |
| | | | |
| | | | |
| | | | |
| | | | |
| | | | |
| | | | |
| | | | |
| | | | |
| | | | |
| | | | |
| | | | |
| | | | |
| | | | |
| | | | |
| | | | |
| | | | |
| | | | |
| | | | |
| | | | |
| | | | |
| | | | |
| | | | |
| | | | |
| | | | |

# Campaign Manager

twitter MARKETING

## Product / Service Campaign

| | |
|---|---|
| Campaign | |
| Description | |
| Product / Service Newsletter<br>Contest / Giveaway | |
| Start | End |
| Objective | |
| Target Audience | |
| Budget$ / Cost$ / Return$ | |
| Landing Page | |
| Tracking Link | |
| Days and Time | |
| Winner / Date Notified | |

Image

- ☐ Blog Post Announcement
- ☐ Blog Post Follow-up
- ☐ Autoresponder Setup
- ☐ Ad Campaign
  - Budget$
  - Cost$
  - Return$
  - Click Thru Rate
  - CPC (Cost per Click)
- ☐ Conversion Rate
- ☐ Hashtag
- ☐ Coupon Code (if applicable)

# Advertising Campaign

| | |
|---|---|
| Campaign | |
| Boost / Ad | |
| Description | |
| Start | End |
| Objective | |
| Target Audience | |
| Budget$ / Cost Per Day$ | |
| Landing Page | |
| Tracking Link | |

| Text |
|---|
| |

| Demographic |
|---|
| |

| Image |
|---|
| |

# To Do

twitter MARKETING

| | Priority | Completed |
|---|---|---|
| | | |
| | | |
| | | |
| | | |
| | | |
| | | |
| | | |
| | | |
| | | |
| | | |
| | | |
| | | |
| | | |
| | | |
| | | |
| | | |
| | | |
| | | |
| | | |
| | | |
| | | |
| | | |

# Notes

# Editorial Calendar



## Month

| SUNDAY | MONDAY | TUESDAY | WEDNESDAY | THURSDAY | FRIDAY | SATURDAY |
|---|---|---|---|---|---|---|
| | | | | | | |
| | | | | | | |
| | | | | | | |
| | | | | | | |
| | | | | | | |

## Notes

# Success Tracker



## Acknowledge and Celebrate Your Success

Month:

---

Total Followers

---

Post with most engagement (Retweets, Favorites, and Replies) on Twitter

---

Post with most clicks

---

Blog post with most traffic from Twitter

---

This month I learned

---

A record I broke this month

---

My celebration this month

---

Next month I plan to do the same

---

Next month I plan to try (new)

---

# Monthly Stats

**GOAL:**

| Total Followers | New Followers | # of Posts | # of Retweets | # of Favorites | # of Comments | # of Mentions | # of Clicks | # of Clicks to Website |
|---|---|---|---|---|---|---|---|---|
| | | | | | | | | |

| | |
|---|---|
| **EMAIL SUBSCRIBERS FROM TWITTER** | |
| **ENGAGEMENT** | |
| **Post with most retweets** | |
| **Post with most favorites** | |
| **Post with most comments** | |
| **Post with most clicks** | |
| **TWITTER ADS** | |

| | | | |
|---|---|---|---|
| Spend $ | | Results | |

# Status Updates



| Twitter Status Updates | Date | Time | ✓ |
|---|---|---|---|
| | | | |
| | | | |
| | | | |
| | | | |
| | | | |
| | | | |
| | | | |
| | | | |
| | | | |
| | | | |
| | | | |
| | | | |
| | | | |
| | | | |
| | | | |
| | | | |
| | | | |
| | | | |
| | | | |
| | | | |
| | | | |
| | | | |
| | | | |
| | | | |
| | | | |
| | | | |
| | | | |

# Campaign Manager

twitter MARKETING

## Product / Service Campaign

| | |
|---|---|
| Campaign | |
| Description | |
| Product / Service Newsletter<br>Contest / Giveaway | |
| Start | End |
| Objective | |
| Target Audience | |
| Budget$ / Cost$ / Return$ | |
| Landing Page | |
| Tracking Link | |
| Days and Time | |
| Winner / Date Notified | |

| Image |
|---|
| |

- ☐ Blog Post Announcement
- ☐ Blog Post Follow-up
- ☐ Autoresponder Setup
- ☐ Ad Campaign
  - Budget$
  - Cost$
  - Return$
  - Click Thru Rate
  - CPC (Cost per Click)
- ☐ Conversion Rate
- ☐ Hashtag
- ☐ Coupon Code (if applicable)

twitter MARKETING

# Advertising Campaign

| | |
|---|---|
| Campaign | |
| Boost / Ad | |
| Description | |
| Start | End |
| Objective | |
| Target Audience | |
| Budget$ / Cost Per Day$ | |
| Landing Page | |
| Tracking Link | |

Text

Demographic

Image

# To Do

twitter MARKETING

| | Priority | Completed |
|---|---|---|
| | | |
| | | |
| | | |
| | | |
| | | |
| | | |
| | | |
| | | |
| | | |
| | | |
| | | |
| | | |
| | | |
| | | |
| | | |
| | | |
| | | |
| | | |
| | | |
| | | |
| | | |
| | | |

# Notes

# Editorial Calendar

twitter MARKETING

## Month

| SUNDAY | MONDAY | TUESDAY | WEDNESDAY | THURSDAY | FRIDAY | SATURDAY |
| --- | --- | --- | --- | --- | --- | --- |
| | | | | | | |
| | | | | | | |
| | | | | | | |
| | | | | | | |
| | | | | | | |

## Notes

# Success Tracker

twitter MARKETING

## Acknowledge and Celebrate Your Success

Month:

Total Followers

Post with most engagement (Retweets, Favorites, and Replies) on Twitter

Post with most clicks

Blog post with most traffic from Twitter

This month I learned

A record I broke this month

My celebration this month

Next month I plan to do the same

Next month I plan to try (new)

# Monthly Stats

GOAL:

| Total Followers | New Followers | # of Posts | # of Retweets | # of Favorites | # of Comments | # of Mentions | # of Clicks | # of Clicks to Website |
|---|---|---|---|---|---|---|---|---|
| | | | | | | | | |

| | |
|---|---|
| **EMAIL SUBSCRIBERS FROM TWITTER** | |
| **ENGAGEMENT** | |
| **Post with most retweets** | |
| **Post with most favorites** | |
| **Post with most comments** | |
| **Post with most clicks** | |
| **TWITTER ADS** | |

| | | | |
|---|---|---|---|
| Spend $ | | Results | |

# Status Updates



| Twitter Status Updates | Date | Time | ✓ |
|---|---|---|---|
| | | | |
| | | | |
| | | | |
| | | | |
| | | | |
| | | | |
| | | | |
| | | | |
| | | | |
| | | | |
| | | | |
| | | | |
| | | | |
| | | | |
| | | | |
| | | | |
| | | | |
| | | | |
| | | | |
| | | | |
| | | | |
| | | | |
| | | | |
| | | | |
| | | | |
| | | | |
| | | | |

# Campaign Manager

twitter MARKETING

## Product / Service Campaign

| | |
|---|---|
| Campaign | |
| Description | |
| Product / Service Newsletter<br>Contest / Giveaway | |
| Start | End |
| Objective | |
| Target Audience | |
| Budget$ / Cost$ / Return$ | |
| Landing Page | |
| Tracking Link | |
| Days and Time | |
| Winner / Date Notified | |

Image

- ☐ Blog Post Announcement
- ☐ Blog Post Follow-up
- ☐ Autoresponder Setup
- ☐ Ad Campaign
  - Budget$
  - Cost$
  - Return$
  - Click Thru Rate
  - CPC (Cost per Click)
- ☐ Conversion Rate
- ☐ Hashtag
- ☐ Coupon Code (if applicable)

# Advertising Campaign

| | |
|---|---|
| Campaign | |
| Boost / Ad | |
| Description | |
| Start | End |
| Objective | |
| Target Audience | |
| Budget$ / Cost Per Day$ | |
| Landing Page | |
| Tracking Link | |

| Text | Demographic |
|---|---|
| | |

| Image |
|---|
| |

# To Do



| | Priority | Completed |
|---|---|---|
| | | |
| | | |
| | | |
| | | |
| | | |
| | | |
| | | |
| | | |
| | | |
| | | |
| | | |
| | | |
| | | |
| | | |
| | | |
| | | |
| | | |
| | | |
| | | |
| | | |
| | | |
| | | |

# Notes

# Editorial Calendar

twitter MARKETING

## Month

| SUNDAY | MONDAY | TUESDAY | WEDNESDAY | THURSDAY | FRIDAY | SATURDAY |
|---|---|---|---|---|---|---|
| | | | | | | |
| | | | | | | |
| | | | | | | |
| | | | | | | |
| | | | | | | |

## Notes

# Success Tracker

## Acknowledge and Celebrate Your Success

Month:

---

Total Followers

---

Post with most engagement (Retweets, Favorites, and Replies) on Twitter

---

Post with most clicks

---

Blog post with most traffic from Twitter

---

This month I learned

---

A record I broke this month

---

My celebration this month

---

Next month I plan to do the same

---

Next month I plan to try (new)

---

# Monthly Stats

GOAL:

| Total Followers | New Followers | # of Posts | # of Retweets | # of Favorites | # of Comments | # of Mentions | # of Clicks | # of Clicks to Website |
|---|---|---|---|---|---|---|---|---|
| | | | | | | | | |

| | |
|---|---|
| **EMAIL SUBSCRIBERS FROM TWITTER** | |
| **ENGAGEMENT** | |
| **Post with most retweets** | |
| **Post with most favorites** | |
| **Post with most comments** | |
| **Post with most clicks** | |
| **TWITTER ADS** | |

| | | | |
|---|---|---|---|
| Spend $ | | Results | |

# Status Updates



| Twitter Status Updates | Date | Time | ✓ |
|---|---|---|---|
| | | | |
| | | | |
| | | | |
| | | | |
| | | | |
| | | | |
| | | | |
| | | | |
| | | | |
| | | | |
| | | | |
| | | | |
| | | | |
| | | | |
| | | | |
| | | | |
| | | | |
| | | | |
| | | | |
| | | | |
| | | | |
| | | | |
| | | | |
| | | | |
| | | | |
| | | | |
| | | | |

# Campaign Manager

twitter MARKETING

## Product / Service Campaign

| | |
|---|---|
| Campaign | |
| Description | |
| Product / Service Newsletter<br>Contest / Giveaway | |
| Start | End |
| Objective | |
| Target Audience | |
| Budget$ / Cost$ / Return$ | |
| Landing Page | |
| Tracking Link | |
| Days and Time | |
| Winner / Date Notified | |

Image

- ☐ Blog Post Announcement
- ☐ Blog Post Follow-up
- ☐ Autoresponder Setup
- ☐ Ad Campaign
  - Budget$
  - Cost$
  - Return$
  - Click Thru Rate
  - CPC (Cost per Click)
- ☐ Conversion Rate
- ☐ Hashtag
- ☐ Coupon Code (if applicable)

# Advertising Campaign

| | |
|---|---|
| Campaign | |
| Boost / Ad | |
| Description | |
| Start | End |
| Objective | |
| Target Audience | |
| Budget$ / Cost Per Day$ | |
| Landing Page | |
| Tracking Link | |

| Text |
|---|
| |

| Demographic |
|---|
| |

| Image |
|---|
| |

# To Do

twitter MARKETING

| | Priority | Completed |
|---|---|---|
| | | |
| | | |
| | | |
| | | |
| | | |
| | | |
| | | |
| | | |
| | | |
| | | |
| | | |
| | | |
| | | |
| | | |
| | | |
| | | |
| | | |
| | | |
| | | |
| | | |
| | | |
| | | |

# Editorial Calendar

twitter MARKETING

## Month

| SUNDAY | MONDAY | TUESDAY | WEDNESDAY | THURSDAY | FRIDAY | SATURDAY |
|---|---|---|---|---|---|---|
| | | | | | | |
| | | | | | | |
| | | | | | | |
| | | | | | | |
| | | | | | | |

## Notes

# Success Tracker

twitter MARKETING

## Acknowledge and Celebrate Your Success

Month:

Total Followers

Post with most engagement (Retweets, Favorites, and Replies) on Twitter

Post with most clicks

Blog post with most traffic from Twitter

This month I learned

A record I broke this month

My celebration this month

Next month I plan to do the same

Next month I plan to try (new)

# Monthly Stats



**GOAL:**

| Total Followers | New Followers | # of Posts | # of Retweets | # of Favorites | # of Comments | # of Mentions | # of Clicks | # of Clicks to Website |
|---|---|---|---|---|---|---|---|---|
| | | | | | | | | |

| | |
|---|---|
| **EMAIL SUBSCRIBERS FROM TWITTER** | |
| **ENGAGEMENT** | |
| **Post with most retweets** | |
| **Post with most favorites** | |
| **Post with most comments** | |
| **Post with most clicks** | |

| | | | |
|---|---|---|---|
| **TWITTER ADS** | | | |
| Spend $ | | Results | |

# Status Updates



| Twitter Status Updates | Date | Time | ✓ |
|---|---|---|---|
| | | | |
| | | | |
| | | | |
| | | | |
| | | | |
| | | | |
| | | | |
| | | | |
| | | | |
| | | | |
| | | | |
| | | | |
| | | | |
| | | | |
| | | | |
| | | | |
| | | | |
| | | | |
| | | | |
| | | | |
| | | | |
| | | | |
| | | | |
| | | | |
| | | | |
| | | | |
| | | | |

# Product / Service Campaign

| | |
|---|---|
| Campaign | |
| Description | |
| Product / Service Newsletter<br>Contest / Giveaway | |
| Start | End |
| Objective | |
| Target Audience | |
| Budget$ / Cost$ / Return$ | |
| Landing Page | |
| Tracking Link | |
| Days and Time | |
| Winner / Date Notified | |

| Image |
|---|
| |

- ☐ Blog Post Announcement
- ☐ Blog Post Follow-up
- ☐ Autoresponder Setup
- ☐ Ad Campaign
  - Budget$
  - Cost$
  - Return$
  - Click Thru Rate
  - CPC (Cost per Click)
- ☐ Conversion Rate
- ☐ Hashtag
- ☐ Coupon Code (if applicable)

# Advertising Campaign

| | |
|---|---|
| Campaign | |
| Boost / Ad | |
| Description | |
| Start | End |
| Objective | |
| Target Audience | |
| Budget$ / Cost Per Day$ | |
| Landing Page | |
| Tracking Link | |

Text

Demographic

Image

# To Do

twitter MARKETING

| | Priority | Completed |
|---|---|---|
| | | |
| | | |
| | | |
| | | |
| | | |
| | | |
| | | |
| | | |
| | | |
| | | |
| | | |
| | | |
| | | |
| | | |
| | | |
| | | |
| | | |
| | | |
| | | |
| | | |
| | | |
| | | |

# Notes

# Editorial Calendar

twitter MARKETING

## Month

| SUNDAY | MONDAY | TUESDAY | WEDNESDAY | THURSDAY | FRIDAY | SATURDAY |
|---|---|---|---|---|---|---|
| | | | | | | |
| | | | | | | |
| | | | | | | |
| | | | | | | |
| | | | | | | |

## Notes

# Success Tracker



## Acknowledge and Celebrate Your Success

Month:

Total Followers

Post with most engagement (Retweets, Favorites, and Replies) on Twitter

Post with most clicks

Blog post with most traffic from Twitter

This month I learned

A record I broke this month

My celebration this month

Next month I plan to do the same

Next month I plan to try (new)

# Monthly Stats

GOAL:

| Total Followers | New Followers | # of Posts | # of Retweets | # of Favorites | # of Comments | # of Mentions | # of Clicks | # of Clicks to Website |
|---|---|---|---|---|---|---|---|---|
| | | | | | | | | |

| | |
|---|---|
| **EMAIL SUBSCRIBERS FROM TWITTER** | |
| **ENGAGEMENT** | |
| **Post with most retweets** | |
| **Post with most favorites** | |
| **Post with most comments** | |
| **Post with most clicks** | |
| **TWITTER ADS** | |

| | | | |
|---|---|---|---|
| Spend $ | | Results | |

| Twitter Status Updates | Date | Time | ✓ |
|---|---|---|---|
| | | | |
| | | | |
| | | | |
| | | | |
| | | | |
| | | | |
| | | | |
| | | | |
| | | | |
| | | | |
| | | | |
| | | | |
| | | | |
| | | | |
| | | | |
| | | | |
| | | | |
| | | | |
| | | | |
| | | | |
| | | | |
| | | | |
| | | | |
| | | | |
| | | | |
| | | | |
| | | | |

# Campaign Manager

twitter MARKETING

## Product / Service Campaign

| | |
|---|---|
| Campaign | |
| Description | |
| Product / Service Newsletter<br>Contest / Giveaway | |
| Start | End |
| Objective | |
| Target Audience | |
| Budget$ / Cost$ / Return$ | |
| Landing Page | |
| Tracking Link | |
| Days and Time | |
| Winner / Date Notified | |

Image

- ☐ Blog Post Announcement
- ☐ Blog Post Follow-up
- ☐ Autoresponder Setup
- ☐ Ad Campaign
  - Budget$
  - Cost$
  - Return$
  - Click Thru Rate
  - CPC (Cost per Click)
- ☐ Conversion Rate
- ☐ Hashtag
- ☐ Coupon Code (if applicable)

# Advertising Campaign

| | |
|---|---|
| Campaign | |
| Boost / Ad | |
| Description | |
| Start | End |
| Objective | |
| Target Audience | |
| Budget$ / Cost Per Day$ | |
| Landing Page | |
| Tracking Link | |

| Text |
|---|
| |

| Demographic |
|---|
| |

| Image |
|---|
| |

# To Do

twitter
MARKETING

| | Priority | Completed |
|---|---|---|
| | | |
| | | |
| | | |
| | | |
| | | |
| | | |
| | | |
| | | |
| | | |
| | | |
| | | |
| | | |
| | | |
| | | |
| | | |
| | | |
| | | |
| | | |
| | | |
| | | |
| | | |

# Notes

# Editorial Calendar

twitter MARKETING

## Month

| SUNDAY | MONDAY | TUESDAY | WEDNESDAY | THURSDAY | FRIDAY | SATURDAY |
|---|---|---|---|---|---|---|
| | | | | | | |
| | | | | | | |
| | | | | | | |
| | | | | | | |
| | | | | | | |

## Notes

# Acknowledge and Celebrate Your Success

Month:

Total Followers

Post with most engagement (Retweets, Favorites, and Replies) on Twitter

Post with most clicks

Blog post with most traffic from Twitter

This month I learned

A record I broke this month

My celebration this month

Next month I plan to do the same

Next month I plan to try (new)

# Monthly Stats

GOAL:

| Total Followers | New Followers | # of Posts | # of Retweets | # of Favorites | # of Comments | # of Mentions | # of Clicks | # of Clicks to Website |
|---|---|---|---|---|---|---|---|---|
| | | | | | | | | |

| | |
|---|---|
| **EMAIL SUBSCRIBERS FROM TWITTER** | |
| **ENGAGEMENT** | |
| **Post with most retweets** | |
| **Post with most favorites** | |
| **Post with most comments** | |
| **Post with most clicks** | |
| **TWITTER ADS** | |

| | | | |
|---|---|---|---|
| Spend $ | | Results | |

# Status Updates



| Twitter Status Updates | Date | Time | ✓ |
|---|---|---|---|
| | | | |
| | | | |
| | | | |
| | | | |
| | | | |
| | | | |
| | | | |
| | | | |
| | | | |
| | | | |
| | | | |
| | | | |
| | | | |
| | | | |
| | | | |
| | | | |
| | | | |
| | | | |
| | | | |
| | | | |
| | | | |
| | | | |
| | | | |
| | | | |
| | | | |
| | | | |
| | | | |

# Campaign Manager

twitter MARKETING

## Product / Service Campaign

| | |
|---|---|
| Campaign | |
| Description | |
| Product / Service Newsletter<br>Contest / Giveaway | |
| Start | End |
| Objective | |
| Target Audience | |
| Budget$ / Cost$ / Return$ | |
| Landing Page | |
| Tracking Link | |
| Days and Time | |
| Winner / Date Notified | |

Image

- ☐ Blog Post Announcement
- ☐ Blog Post Follow-up
- ☐ Autoresponder Setup
- ☐ Ad Campaign
  - Budget$
  - Cost$
  - Return$
  - Click Thru Rate
  - CPC (Cost per Click)
- ☐ Conversion Rate
- ☐ Hashtag
- ☐ Coupon Code (if applicable)

# Advertising Campaign

| | |
|---|---|
| Campaign | |
| Boost / Ad | |
| Description | |
| Start | End |
| Objective | |
| Target Audience | |
| Budget$ / Cost Per Day$ | |
| Landing Page | |
| Tracking Link | |

Text

Demographic

Image

# To Do



| | Priority | Completed |
|---|---|---|
| | | |
| | | |
| | | |
| | | |
| | | |
| | | |
| | | |
| | | |
| | | |
| | | |
| | | |
| | | |
| | | |
| | | |
| | | |
| | | |
| | | |
| | | |
| | | |
| | | |
| | | |
| | | |

# Notes

# Editorial Calendar

twitter MARKETING

## Month

| SUNDAY | MONDAY | TUESDAY | WEDNESDAY | THURSDAY | FRIDAY | SATURDAY |
|---|---|---|---|---|---|---|
| | | | | | | |
| | | | | | | |
| | | | | | | |
| | | | | | | |
| | | | | | | |

## Notes

# Success Tracker



## Acknowledge and Celebrate Your Success

Month:

---

Total Followers

---

Post with most engagement (Retweets, Favorites, and Replies) on Twitter

---

Post with most clicks

---

Blog post with most traffic from Twitter

---

This month I learned

---

A record I broke this month

---

My celebration this month

---

Next month I plan to do the same

---

Next month I plan to try (new)

---

# Monthly Stats



**GOAL:**

| Total Followers | New Followers | # of Posts | # of Retweets | # of Favorites | # of Comments | # of Mentions | # of Clicks | # of Clicks to Website |
|---|---|---|---|---|---|---|---|---|
| | | | | | | | | |

| | |
|---|---|
| **EMAIL SUBSCRIBERS FROM TWITTER** | |
| **ENGAGEMENT** | |
| **Post with most retweets** | |
| **Post with most favorites** | |
| **Post with most comments** | |
| **Post with most clicks** | |

| | | | |
|---|---|---|---|
| **TWITTER ADS** | | | |
| Spend $ | | Results | |

| Twitter Status Updates | Date | Time | ✓ |
|---|---|---|---|
| | | | |
| | | | |
| | | | |
| | | | |
| | | | |
| | | | |
| | | | |
| | | | |
| | | | |
| | | | |
| | | | |
| | | | |
| | | | |
| | | | |
| | | | |
| | | | |
| | | | |
| | | | |
| | | | |
| | | | |
| | | | |
| | | | |
| | | | |
| | | | |
| | | | |
| | | | |
| | | | |

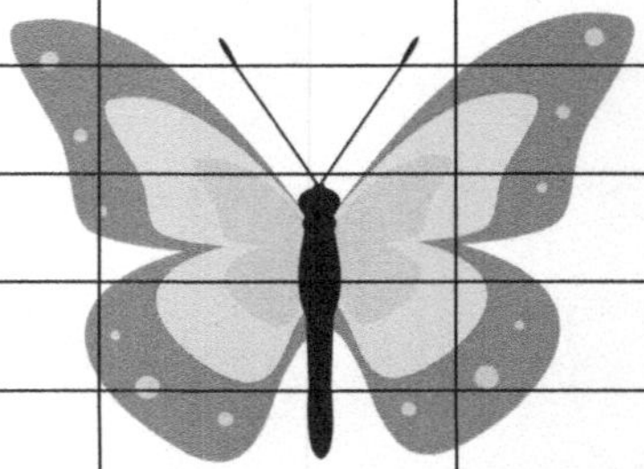

# Campaign Manager

twitter MARKETING

## Product / Service Campaign

| | |
|---|---|
| Campaign | |
| Description | |
| Product / Service Newsletter<br>Contest / Giveaway | |
| Start | End |
| Objective | |
| Target Audience | |
| Budget$ / Cost$ / Return$ | |
| Landing Page | |
| Tracking Link | |
| Days and Time | |
| Winner / Date Notified | |

| Image |
|---|
| |

- ☐ Blog Post Announcement
- ☐ Blog Post Follow-up
- ☐ Autoresponder Setup
- ☐ Ad Campaign
  - Budget$
  - Cost$
  - Return$
  - Click Thru Rate
  - CPC (Cost per Click)
- ☐ Conversion Rate
- ☐ Hashtag
- ☐ Coupon Code (if applicable)

# Campaign Manager

twitter MARKETING

## Advertising Campaign

| | |
|---|---|
| Campaign | |
| Boost / Ad | |
| Description | |
| Start | End |
| Objective | |
| Target Audience | |
| Budget$ / Cost Per Day$ | |
| Landing Page | |
| Tracking Link | |

| Text | Demographic |
|---|---|
| | |
| | Image |
| | |

# To Do



| | Priority | Completed |
| --- | --- | --- |
| | | |
| | | |
| | | |
| | | |
| | | |
| | | |
| | | |
| | | |
| | | |
| | | |
| | | |
| | | |
| | | |
| | | |
| | | |
| | | |
| | | |
| | | |
| | | |
| | | |
| | | |

HOPE YOU ENJOYED USING
YOUR TWITTER WORKBOOK AND PLANNER

**GET YOUR FREE WEEKLY TWITTER PLANNER!**
http://bit.ly/twitterweekly

PLEASE LEAVE A REVIEW ON AMAZON

BE SURE TO GRAB YOUR COPIES
**- Social Media Marketing Workbook -**
**- Social Media Marketing Planner -**
**- Google+ Workbook and Planner -**
**- LinkedIn Workbook and Planner -**
**- Facebook Workbook and Planner -**
**- Pinterest Workbook and Planner -**
**- Instagram Workbook and Planner -**

ALSO LOOK OUT FOR
*Authentic Marketing – The Three E's of Online Marketing: Ethical, Effortless, Engaging*
*Social Media Marketing: How to Master Engagement in 15 Minutes a Day.*

Connect with Dwainia Grey on LinkedIn, Google+, Facebook, Twitter, Pinterest and Instagram
dwainiagrey.me